Also by Stephen Ratcliffe

Some Time

Poems 1970 - 1980

Stephen Ratcliffe

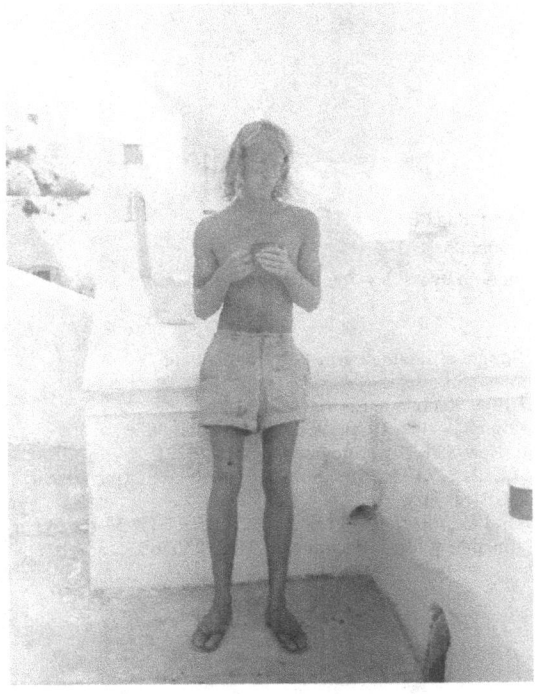

Spuyten Duyvil
New York City

Some of these poems have appeared in:

The Compass, The Greensboro Review, The Massachusetts Review, Meadowlark, Occident, On the Mesa: An Anthology of Bolinas Writing, Poetry, Prairie Schooner, and The Southern Review.

© 2022 Stephen Ratcliffe
ISBN 978-1-956005-38-7
Cover photograph by Ashley Ratcliffe, Santorini Greece, 1972

Library of Congress Cataloging-in-Publication Data

Names: Ratcliffe, Stephen, author.
Title: Some time : poems, 1970-1980 / Stephen Ratcliffe.
Description: New York city : Spuyten Duyvil, [2022]
Identifiers: LCCN 2021056565 | ISBN 9781956005387 (paperback)
Subjects: LCGFT: Poetry.
Classification: LCC PS3568.A717 S65 2022 | DDC 811/.54--dc23/eng/20211220
LC record available at https://lccn.loc.gov/2021056565

For Ashley and Oona

Contents

Some Time

The Eagle's Song

The sun ray
lies in my wings
before dawn
    O in my wings
tight in the long feathers
it lies, the day
slow to begin.

    *

My shadow turns
thinned as I lift
at high noon
    O as I shift
light in the wind circling
it turns, the shade
gathering in.

    *

The dark earth
falls in the sky
at sun down
    O in my eye
night in the near distance
it falls, a sphere
west of the sun.

Waterfall

Over glacial smooth granite
the current sweeps
as it must, swift
in the white rush of winter.

Yellowed leaves of the aspen
have raced here, down
with purling drops
that are spilled sounding the air.

Now, in a cleft, where the pool
is still, the leaves
under ice lie
stained in watery cold,

and at the falls, ringed against
the deepened chill
of the blue, clear
sluice pours itself in the glare.

El Capitan

Fingers delicately stretched,
the climber moves high
between rock and sky
his senses keyed to the touch

of natural crack that winds
up far from sight,
cut against the height,
the stone immutable and blind.

Compelled to fix his stay, he
is kept by the rare
aspect of air
that grazes, imperceptibly,

the granite face and his cheek.
Men wander below,
out of sound; the blow
of stillness is cold and bleak

on the sill, until he rings
that solitude of sheer
space, by striking clear,
to steel, as the piton sings.

Readings from John Muir's Journal

With eyes of the owl
and the jay's cry
I wake in the open air

to the slow of new day—
light in the oak & yellow pine,
the stream running into my ears.

                    *

Maple leaves from a winter
or two, or six,
dry cracked
    my voice, my foot
the measure of my climb.

*

Noon. The mid March
sun begins
to penetrate my

skin, my bones, begins
to warm the lake
side where

waterlichen
has gripped down
for so long.

*

The metaphysis of Indian
red madrone to drift
wood, riverwood, run

& weathered, the slow
decay, the sigh
of a time not mine.

*

April 4: the silver fir,
the light, the Merced
dropping over the falls,

the embroidered spray,
the sight, thunder
rolling from the height.

*

This cowslip, violet
deep at the stem, to sky
blue, to the jade

behind startips pointed
in a ring,
to no sound at all.

*

At the saddle ridgecrest,
where shade will come long
& cold, two deer,

California mule, graze
in the half light,
ears cocked, listening

*

Late afternoon on the Sawyer
Camp Road, the wind
down on the lake,

the water deeply green,
the mating of ducks shrill
in the splash, there.

                        *

Mosaic was the weight
of the sun,
          these
eyes in the blue
light of the sea,
                le ciel,
the wild
        of twilight—iris
blue in the curl
                & lash.

                        *

The full moon falling
all around me drips
from honeysuckle

leaftips to petals
where it pools in drops
casting a moonlit spell.

*

Across the way, rising
from a crest of pinetops,
a crystal sky full

of first magnitude stars
drifts, in flight, above
the sleeping, shadowed night.

The View from Mono Pass

Luminous peaks, the
azure dome of noon
above a distant

range, the rapid sound
of wind on stone so
simplified. Below,

lost in the hollow
glare, the sound of a
circling red-tailed hawk—

soft wings dividing
the air above the
shadowed, granite rock

upon which, stopping
to rest where water
steeps through tufted green

and spills upon the
lichen crest, the rat,
hesitant, is seen.

Pause, Pico Blanco

Through mountain hush
noise in the brush—
an earth-brown deer
bounds into clear

open spaces.
In its place is
the bone-dry grass.
And so we pass.

Summer Rain

Bending each grass, the warm wind fills
these undulant dry coastal hills

with ocean moisture which the sea,
welling in grey-washed clouds, distills

into a salt humidity.
Unseasonable rain is near—

in tawny distant atmosphere
like an elusive shaft of light

is nearly falling. Still, I hear
insects intensify their flight.

The Snake

In the cool green
light the creeping

vines jingle like
soft bells damped in

velvet. It is
raining and you

are the naked
original

Eve about to
slip. A tendril

curled under your
foot and around

your long, slender
ankle with a

tongue soft as
coral and eyes

is not the snake.
I am lurking

elsewhere, perhaps
in the coiling

orchid under
your other ear.

The Rat

These ladies say "Ted
Roethke's rat is dead.
It is dead." The word
passes under wet

stones, a corpse slightly
stiff with the malaise
of gossip, the stench
of fear crusted on

dry tongues. Already
the oak cellars are
mellower, the wombs
impregnable, now

that we see how soon
the unruly are
paid. Put away your
black scarves. The children
are safe. It is dead.

Logging

I am almost
ready. The great
hawthorn spreads
quietly with soft
grey flecks of cloud
behind her dark
leaves, her branches
reaching like wild
green tentacles
20,000
leagues under the
moonlit sea. I
scarcely know how
I'll manage this
affair. Everyone
in the crowd waits
on pins so I've
got to get on
with it only
no matter how
hard I swing her
voice keeps calling
thou shall not kill.

Blood

The sandhill cranes in
flight like swallows and
other small birds have
learned to rely on
instinct. That is why
when they get up or
rather wheel into
the cold, Canada

dawn knowing South is
neither tundra, tall-
wood nor yellowing
steppe they drive further,
over floating earth,
gorging the air's blood.

Rustic Diversions

From a winnower of corn to the winds

Angels on wing,
sunlight rising
over earth-spin,
as meadowland
flowers in fanned
shadow begin,

I give you these—
lilac, lilies,
a flushing rose
as sweet to kiss,
ready as this
flesh to enclose.

So sweet breath turn
and breathing burn
my plain today:
meadow is sown,
unflower flown
in seed away.

after Joachim du Bellay

*

            Past, the present
seems to compose
decay begins
to press to-
wards in re-
memb'ring pose
                me
flow'ring again:

fills the future
coverful past-
oral please
              re-
lease the near
distances back
& forth nearly
suffice except
when do you know. . .

        so tell me
ever truly
lady amuse
me who came yes-
terdays my moon-
light
        made by eve-
ning everything
as before you
forgot Past
                & yet
now, where is it?

*

Earth dies quickly
come for pleasure
away
    anchors
cut by the free
swinging your blade . . .

soft as sever
the entrance in
to seas
      leaping
froth like dolphins
prow to engulf—

then only blue
to deliver
alive
    the earth
seasoned with men
stilled for changing:

hymns will sing for-
giving you search
for pearls
     shimmer
filled you fathom
the sounding done.

*

Gone, by name recall
gardens of
            roses where
when winter was
fielding & full
with chorus
            now you
count sweetly ruin. . .

late then was new leaf
returning not
            before but
after the bud
begins believe
the coming
            hence can
come never undone:

in song soon we find
nesting again
            birds &
unburdened past
springs behind
each eyelid
            on wings en-
laced with delight.

*

Planting

Over crowding
every word we
watch
    list'ing
how they lean
forward & now
reverse

      Progress
sows the seed back
handed down by row
line by
    line learns
tradition is found
returning.

      Thus to cultivate
cover that keeps the seedling
deep you shovel
      over them care
fully soils & under: for till
lies in ground ready to come.

Flight

Yesterday I vanished,
lifting like a bird,
fled upon the English
island's lovely word

not divine direction,
nonetheless by plan—
bold Atlantic Ocean
my familiar man,

London like a riddle,
Thames the silver swan,
shades in continental
Europe lit by dawn—
nothing but to travel
then, to come upon.

Concert, London

In the Lyceum the lights
are glowing slowly greener.

Already your senses are
confused, already gather

together against your head
as the live, electric Dead

begin to exact their fees
of admission. Soon, only

the most courageous will be
able to see such delights.

Air

Silent music—
the empty

space
behind

Campion's
words on the page.

Gioconda

Hand upon hand, fingers,
part of a motion
back, roadways, where
do you winding flow
we wonder

      whose the eyes
are, so dark, so
nearly disguised
their darkness seems to
leap from the lighter
distances, come with
almost a vengeance
whether to

      know you, skin
you, kiss the bare
bone, or else once
to be known, discovered
themselves in stripped
back the canvas back
the warmed flesh
darkened with

      fear, or
was it amusement merely
shadowed, a vanishing
smile that keeps them
close to the colder greens?

Still Life

With cherries you never know just how
to begin. Do you
raise them against
the white cirrus, dripping,
or place them just so your eye
can catch in each burgundy globe
the light, or else just leave them
alone, in a basket, washed, the still
life you imagined Cézanne might make,
where the basket itself just seems
to be spilling the various small
fruits which themselves simply
pretend to be polished ripe
cherries beginning
to fall, or just
never beginning to sweetly smear you?

Versailles

I eat only
weeds. The con-
sequence makes
me wonder-

fly like a
French thinman
wearing a chic
chemise or

the second
Sun King Louis
afloat on blue
splendors.

Rome

Is the charm
sprung when
accidents
I am

in the words
like Christ
crucified
converge.

Horologe, Venice

The bellclaps are
two gentlemen
as naked as
Adam often

appears in those
incredible
Italian falls,
only double.

Postscript, On a Name

Ezra Pound (his fingers, bones)
lies beneath Venetian stones,
ivy laced, in lupine bound,
lilac, laurel all around:

Here you read me, here my name—
POUND inscribed in marble fame,
almost breathing, almost brave,
concentrates what Time forgave.

Overland from Trieste

The bus travels across dry
hills rolling into faded

afternoon blues and greens—soft
reclining seats, ample leg

room, Yugoslavian songs
on the radio—welcome

to ranchland California,
circa 1846.

Blues

near Dubrovnik

Deep Dalmatian blues
—air, ocean—confuse

in the warm azure
of mornings on far

off California
beaches, volcanic

rocks descending in
to ultramarine.

Pacheteau's

Calistoga Hot Springs

Shower

I take off my clothes and walk naked
into the room. The showers running
constantly have filled the room with warm
moist air and the walls are mildewing
and the cement floor is old and worn.
The shower itself is made of baked

ceramic tile, dimly lit and worn
smooth by the streams of mineral water
running down its polished surfaces,
water that comes out of a geyser
nearby at 212 degrees—
purified, beneficial, and warm.

*

Mud

It is in great troughs.
A man in white tells
me I can get in.
Hesitating, I
swing myself up, turn,
and settle back down
into it. With his
strong hands he shovels
black mud onto thin
legs, waist, arms, chest and
shoulders until all
that remains of me
is my head, eyes closed,
slowly dissolving
into the warm black mud's
primeval relief.

*

Bath

Old claw-
foot tub,
man getting

down in
to the
water's Good

Morning,
did you
meet my friend

the drowned
(who lies
full fathom

five)
man—
the water's healing heat.

*

Steam

The hole I put
my head through is
the hell hole, man,
black on the in-
side and so wet

I feel myself,
my skin, begin
to sweat, slipping
away, drinking
this liquid air.

*

Bed

Thin little pallet,
floor mud brick red, two
feet high,

white tongue and groove, walls
empty except for
my jeans.

He wraps me up in
clean white towels, blanket
to dry,

and feeds me mineral
water through a straw,
which cleans

my insides out as
equally as out-
sides in.

*

Massage

It is afternoon when I
wake, unroll myself, and step
across to the massage room.
He is, as before, in white.
I climb up onto the long
comfortable table and
he begins rubbing me down
with oil—Achilles tendons,

calves, thighs, buttocks, shoulders, neck—
explaining "It simply helps
stimulate circulation."
Tight muscles loosening as
he works the lubricated
skin, I feel it in my blood.

Kauai

Bali H'ai

Green river valleys,
water and sky blue,
warm tropical air—
is this paradise?
"No more than elsewhere"

the God said, "given
a bird's eye view of
beautiful island
expanses in which
to escape as planned."

*

Swimming at Poipu Beach

Blue wind, blue
water, blue
sea & sky
that is, these
elements
in which I
lose myself
to find-

       "<u>Wind</u>
<u>and water</u>
<u>make a man</u>
<u>smarter</u>"-
          as
Shakespeare's five
fathoms made
the father's
bones coral,

his eyes pearl,
his nothing
that faded
in the sea's
change suffer
into some
precious thing
(sea nymphs ring-
  ing his bells).

               *

Highway 56

Lihue
Kapaia
Wailua
Kapaa

Kealia
Anahola
Kilauea
Kalihiwai Bay

Hanalei Bay
Lumahai
Wainiha
Haena

*

Hiking the Napali Coast

The ancient Hawaiian trail
climbs gradually above
the ultramarine changing
to turquoise of the reef's cove
into a sunlit jungle
where, hanging into space, tall
trees with air roots wave cactus
like fronds bearing pineapple

like flowers-bromeliads
I'm told-beneath a mountain
side which itself seems to move
when the green sea of unknown
tropical foliage blows
above vast, Pacific blues.

*

Departure

Leaving Lihue at 6 A.M.-
jets,
birds,
traffic,
rain-
bows.

South

Muriel

Stopping at the airport
in New Orleans, humid,
temperature in the mid nineties,

two hours to kill enroute
to Mobile. She is there—
your oldest friend become Sister

Muriel (Convent of
the Sacred Heart)—and drives
us through the twilight to visit

the levee above the
river, the late summer
tugboats and barges moving South.

                *

Ida

An antebellum
mansion near Pleasant
Hill, Alabama,
"1825" visible above
one of its columns,
oaks & magnolias
& an overgrown
graveyard out in back,
nobody at home
but the old caretaker
who talks about how it was
back in "slavey times"

*

Billy

Sipping eau de vie de poire
("pear grappa") on the porch last
night with father-in-law,
sudden illumination—
a flash of blue-white lightning
silhouetting pine & oak,
the 3 man-made lakes & his
Creole cottage, a modern
oversized reproduction.

*

Forest Service

Rattlesnake—five foot
diamond back—crossing
a graded red dirt
road cutting between

green pastures: red necks
who work in the woods
drive up behind it,
kill it with a stick.

*

Brentz

Lunch at the country club
with neat golfers
and young girls;

homes on Government Street
razed to make room
for their stuff;

pine forest all around
Spring Hill cleared
for condominiums—

"condohooligans"
brother-in-law grins
and then shrugs.

*

Webb

Since her fingers are swelling
she has taken her rings off.

Otherwise she sits at home
and doesn't remember your

name, why you've come, who she is—
blue veins in paper-thin skin.

*

Uncle Robert

Sand dunes and sea oats,
skipper jacks and blues,
terns, pelicans, cranes,
an old house on poles,
Uncle Robert's place:
swim before coffee,

West Indies salad
for lunch, afternoons
of Winslow Homer
sailing below grey
skies, squalls threatening
on the horizon.

*

Weather

In the early morning
no wind, already warm;
by eleven the breeze
coming easterly or
from the northeast, cooling
the horizon, driving

what little surf there is
on shore, flattening it;
by mid afternoon tall
cumulus piling down
from Baldwin County; at
dusk thunder, heat lightning.

*

Little Lagoon

At its western edge
the white sand margin
doubles as access
to an old Gulf house
built in the twenties;
abandoned, the place

still is beautiful—
the tall stand of pines
across the lagoon,
the fresh water lake
just there, marsh around
it, the trout jumping.

*

Della

She prepares the last
supper. Later, on

the lawn: crickets, roast
lamb, corn pudding, rolls,

black bottom pie, half
moon, September 1.

*

Home

A late afternoon flight
home from Mobile, massive

thunderheads towering
clear to Houston, Phoenix

alive with lights, at mid-
night Bolinas, dreaming.

Aubaude

Good morning my love-
ly dove. Forgive
the deep
sleep.
Wake
me quick-
ly with surprise
in bright, blue eyes.

Lunch

Now let
us get together
over California wine
extra sour French bread
a salad made simply by mixing

salt
pepper
Dijon mustard
vinegar
oil

1 green onion from the garden
parsley from the garden
left over brown rice
a sliced tomato
lettuce.

Interstate 280

Thinking about my wife and baby
amuses me while I drive home
tonight on Interstate 280.

A sea of fog cascading from
green hills, lupine late in April
amuses me while I drive home.

Listening to Mozart and Vivaldi
instead of news, drinking a cold
imported beer, eating some raisins,
thinking about my wife and baby
amuses me while I drive home
tonight on Interstate 280.

The Message

All I want,
peace
and quiet

just a small
space
to breathe

in and out,
in
and out.

The Window

This shining in—
grey light, light rain
falling in April.
Or is spring

I feel myself
falling into
that place I wanted
most to be,

in the garden
the onions all
coming up after
the last frost?

Star Route Farm Journal

Milking

Her calf let
out of the shed,
milk ready

to come down
fast as I
can let it—

hands on her
teats, bucket
between my knees,

my head against her
warm dark side
in the manger.

*

Peas

Picking them fresh
from Weber's field

at the edge
of Paradise

Valley (shorts and
no shirt) I find

the meaning of
"brasero": back

bent, sunburnt, 5
hundred pounds of

peas.

*

Potatoes

A slit gunny sack around
my neck with a 20 lb.

supply of small red and white
potatoes dotted with eyes,

I toss them into a trench
from 12 to 18 inches

apart, then work back along
the furrows raking dark spring

topsoil over them—the plowed
earth about to be planted

*

Now, less than 3 months later,
the plants' soft forest of green

leaves spreading over the ground,
their small purple flowers wet

with dew, we begin to dig
shovel by heavy shovel

full of potatoes tangled
in a mass of roots: russets

pungent as a fresh cut field,
the reds dark, almost blood red.

Garlic

Planting

Cloves staggered along
both sides of the string

8 inches apart,
having broken dirt

clods by hand (thistles
deadly), I finish
with irrigation
pipes, sprinklers set, pump

primed, handle turned "ON"—
then watch the rain shine.

*

Weeding

By hand, in late May, after
a light rain, because they were

planted December 2nd
and haven't been done yet and

who'll do it if I don't, I
crawl down the long rows of root

stalks choked with plantain, purple
vetch, mustard, thistle, wild

geranium, California
poppy and clumps of calla

lily—"foison plenty"—and
sometimes when a tuft of black

wet ground pulls loose catch a glimpse
of where the garlic's giant milk-

white bulb lies swelling, swelling...

*

Hay

Oat seed planted in
early November
in various fields
around here—Bromwell's
on the ridge above
Paradise Valley,
Hamilton's on Horse-
shoe Hill, Tacherra's—

and fed by the sparse
rains of a drought year
comes to this: blond shocks
like small mounds of gold
piled from windrows raked
with an old John Deere.

*

The 4-pronged pitch fork's
prongs rubbed smooth with use,
the dry rustling sound
of hay as I pitch
it over my head
into the pickup,
the haystack building
15 by 20-

5 by 12 feet high
in perfect weather
for hay, overcast—
"you're building a mon-
ument" one man said,
"visible for miles."

Zucchini

Thinning

Again after rain,
"killdeer" alive in
the distances, the
topsoil so moist it
sticks to your shoes, slows
life down to these short

sharp strokes of a hoe
—rusted steel head stuck
  to an old handle—
thinning zucchini
to 2 feet under
grey clouds, 9 A.M.

*

7.7.77

Birthday today, less
than a month after
the first thinning, I
pull apart the large
elephant earlike
leaves (a lime green frog

crouched in one) to find
behind each pumpkin
yellow trumpet shaped
squash blossom the firm
6-inch zucchini
coming into prime.

*

Kelly Box Company

Warm wind city stink
coming into nostrils
stacking one hundred
used boxes ("Flower
Beauty," "Mr. Kal,"
"de Palma & Son")

by 4's—1 under
2 standing back to
back inside it, 1
a lid on top: 4
weeks' zucchini har-
vest on Star Route Farm.

*

Water

Carrying it through
the afternoon heat
in 2-gallon cans
attempting to save
the cucumbers in
late July—the drought

getting worse, Pine Gulch
down to a trickle,
no irrigation
for weeks, zucchini
already going
flaccid without it.

*

Picking

Dragging a small cart
behind filling its
crates of zucchini
with 2 grades "FANCY"
and "MEDIUM"—Net
Contents" 23 lbs.

on days when it's hot
I roll up my sleeves
both arms getting cut
by their spiney stalks
and leaves—soft on top,
prickles underneath

*

camouflaged in that
green jungle yellow
mottled surfaces
bright as the under-
bellies of brook trout,
I slice the young fruit

off with a pocket
knife, leaving the rest
—sea slugs, leeches, black
  suckers, "OVERSIZED"—
too much to market,
"feed-em to the hogs."

Cucumbers

Thinning

This time with a hula hoe,
clouds opening to reveal
celestial blue sky,
I find half a perfect
Indian pestle—round granite
5" long by 2 1/2
at the broken off end,
the head ground smooth,

running the length of it
lighter in color than
the dark dull grey
color of wet
cement, a
shallow blue scratch.

*

Pickles

Early August some
old Mason and Ball
and Le Parfait jars
filled with cucumbers
and fresh picked dill, you
boil up a pot of
vinegar, salt, red
and black pepper and

garlic cloves so sharp
your nose burns, pour it
over them, put the
sealed jars away in
a dark closet (six
months later pickles).

There

chalk bluffs
always there

two orange chairs
as usual

                              *

"maybe this is really a dream"

                              *

"all together with all the things together"

                              *

stream below cabin
chrrrrr of crickets at screen window
the child asleep at last

                              *

"Hi dad

'm making my bed"

                    *

All day
reading proofs
poolside

see the water
bugs

red
pen
tan
hand

sun
oak
shadow

clouds
blow
by

smooth
surface

SPLASH!

rip-
ples

read
"Riddles"

              *

"<u>Daddy</u>
 <u>what are you</u>
 <u>doing</u>"

              *

lifting stones
from the dam

to let steel-
head travel

              *

gin
and
tonics

on the rocks

                    *

PINE
CONE
SPRING

water
crystal
analysis

parts per million
manganese
faint trace

mild laxatives
acid condition
sick headaches

catarrhal conditions
mucous membranes
urinary organs

Merritt 3733

*

"<u>telephone wires
go for miles</u>"

*

PASSING CAR

gone

*

occasional plane
overhead

north to south
south to north

world beyond
BIG CANYON

              *

funny family
up the road

Paula rescues
animals

leaves the kid to
her old man

Carl "you'll never
wake him up"

              *

"get dressed go fishing"

              *

strong tug
from rock

Water-
fall Pool

line, pink
-egg, hook

crayfish
should've been

snagged claw
drop it

*

"I almost catched the president lizard"

*

grass noose

*

random motion of
hundreds of dragonflies
FEEDING!

*

daddy long-legs
making his way

across the wide
linoleum

*

"I love you best of all"

*

girl breaking glass
image of live oak

branches in blue pool
this last evening

*

<u>"I won't die for a long long time"</u>